VIII Stepping Poems & other pieces

Fergal Gaynor

Miami University Press
Oxford, Ohio

New Writers Press
Dublin, Ireland

For those who held space open for words: my father (r.i.p.) and mother, Thomas Lande, Fr. Aengus Fagan (r.i.p.), Patrick Galvin and Mary Johnson, Kevin Perryman, Trevor Joyce and Keith Tuma. And, of course, for Marja.

Poems originally published in *Shearsman, The Journal of Nietzsche Studies, Poetry Salzburg Review, Free Verse, Ping Pong, Masthead, SoundEye Pamphlets, The Gig* and *Maya Recordings mcd 1003.* Thanks to the editors involved.

Library of Congress Cataloging-in-Publication Data

Gaynor, Fergal, 1969-
VIII stepping poems : & other pieces / by Fergal Gaynor ; edited by Keith Tuma.
p. cm.
ISBN-13: 978-1-4507-3710-4
ISBN-10: 1-4507-3710-2
I. Title. II. Title: Eight stepping poems. III. Title: 8 stepping poems.
PR6107.A97A13 2011
821'.92--dc22

2010039626

Contents

VIII Stepping Poems **5**

Various (2002–2005)

Twinning (a Semi-Sestina for the Celtic Tiger) 19
Cork's Lough (for Marja) 20
Angler 24
New Media (for Breda) 25

Runes **27**

Portraits

Elizabeth Bowen 34
Beckett 36
Nietzsche 37

XI Pieces for Austria-Hungary **41**

Various (1999 – 2001)

Seagull 45
The Quarry 46
The Flood (after a Reading by Trevor Joyce and Mike Smith) 47

III Further Stepping Poems **49**

Various (2009–2010)

Ella 56
Idea for a New College (for John Clarke) 56
After J.S. Bach's *Musical Offering* (for Maya and Barry) . . 58

From Lower Realms **64**

VIII Stepping Poems

I.M. Christopher P. Gaynor
Teacher and Philologist
1939–2006

Note: the asterisks between sections denote pauses of differing lengths

I.

Is it the water rising
or the land's extremity?

*

a step, a short leap,
a step, a look, a step

*

before Lyell
Blake like God
inlaying the rock
with vivid remains

*

Dyce's Pegwell Bay
decalcomania
so soon

*

as the apparatus advances
the mountain approximates
a shape
(a shape is that
which may be wiped away)

*

seashape
sealanguage
wind mixed
seaflag

*

footfeeling

*

the invisible hand

II.

The college library
rumbles like a ship
each book
telling of an island
but there is only sea
night sea
with moving stars

*

young oaks
happily shaking
young leaves

*

it is said
that at his touch
the worn Virgil
would leave its perch
opening on the page
with the apposite line

*

a block
a blind man
a tongue that will not respond
these too

*

catastrophe
stranger still
continuation

*

stella orbis
bright gap

between etched
non-rays

*

and then again

III.

We develop
apartment

*

so body entered machine
machine entered body
so issued
a haunted bureau

*

the river
oily
slow as a snake
on the bank
shafts of ebony
in the undergrowth
atmosphere of coffee
the oleograph
of Reynolds' 'Girl'
a travel-bag marked
TWA

*

small adjustments
in the bathroom
a bar
for support

*

their last retreat
where memory
is inseparable
from dream

*

and then the sound
inside outside
the sound
of a wind rising

*

where it leaves off on the air

IV.

Dry commotion
a cast of bones

*

what?
would you burn
shadows?

*

evening lights the fires
so under the northern star
sign of endurance
the inner life opens
the characters line up

*

you
the first time
by a wrought-iron gate

among laurels
among yews

*

echoes
the afterlife

*

on the water's surface
sunstrikes
gathering

*

NOW

V.

Unnamed
you will be invisible
the invisible
is without protection
named
you will be visible
the visible
is at their disposal

*

music
like night
in the shell's ear

*

the needle jumps
to a holler from the Deep South
children of slaves
children of hard labour
yawps and howls to claim
the first electric fields

*

it was weighed
and happily found
wanting more

*

I met Apollo in the woods today
the Delian was in a laurel bush
I almost passed him quite unaware
so slight
his presence has become
a sibilance
in the leaves like thin breathing
no not breath
the light catch
preceding inspiration
stopped me
and I addressed the god saying

*

exchange of space
rapid changeable oarings
of the last rower
marooned in air

*

where was I?

*

out

VI.

It has spoken
through the profits

*

each wing moving
contrarily to the other
so that the bird
spins
becomes an engine
or a blind dart

*

broken-backed
yet living

*

'Have you any jobs for a teacher?'
He is eighty-seven. This is a hospital.
'You teach Irish?'
'I do.'
Never yes or no. Always stress or inflection.
'I teach English myself. I cannot get a job.'
'That's bad.'
My move was poor.
'But then they're often looking for Irish
teachers. You're more likely to get a job
teaching Irish.'
'You could be right.'
Then –
'All we can do is hope.'
After which I turn away, happy that my
my oracle has again delivered. At this he
repeats, as if I had not listened:
'Hope.'

*

beyond the bird partition
in the kitchen

yellow whistling

*

prenez soin Francis
des pommes de terre!

*

on a wave of blood
I am delivered here
my shape remembers
each stage of creation

VII.

Development
emergency
resistance

*

Rome's Pantheon
capped with concrete cosmos
it has a hole
through which rain falls
long way
to the mosaiced floor

*

the plain of Tipperary
at vespers
ringed with gold
the bright ones
on the horizon
the earth bright
lifting its fertility
from it
comes

to it
returns
as the morning was long
so the evening
the day was short
a wind has risen
blowing through the mountains
reverse of
a halting
breath
a-n-i-m-a

*

borne helpless
Anchises
beloved of the goddess
what images filled his eyes
directed to lurid seas?

*

the town bypassed
soon stagnates

*

by the new's appearance
the shock has already been
weird tones released
from the shuddering frame
ah! schmecht gut!

*

drive

VIII.

Birches and social housing
kodak of perpetual spring

*

the homeland
in care
of familiar machines
machines manned
by engineers
like your father
he attends
the turning airport beam
even in that hour
when you wake
and look through mullioned windows
onto a silent suburban street

*

what we have left
of us
is suffering

*

incursion of light
afterwards
the task of building
in light's stone carcass

*

yet again
you have looked into the open
and seen your changed reflection
there
where your eye is swallowed

black hole
still point of the moving
whatever:
emergency endless
collapse into rigour

*

sunt lacrimae
soft filigree of tears
reticule of tears shifting
on a rising salt tide
of what had once been
one tear
then another
tear after tear
dissolving
this fabric of forms
given to the wash
washing salt waters
of tear after tear after tear
being
submerged
as the tide rises
as the tears tear
until
exhaustion
and all
a shifting tear-surface
soft-waved in sunlight
breeze-touched
where newborn love
prepares her lexicon
fathoms above

the misshapen bed
its shadowy monuments

Various (2002 – 2005)

Twinning

Créad í an ruaig so ar thoraibh
Buala buan a mbona?
(What is this human tumult
with so much fell destruction?)

Shandon tower
that grand old dame
stript of her decorous urns
shall earth never sleep?
the jackhammers strike no
though Murphy nods
and Mahony and Mahood
seeds in the shifting ground
knowing nor 'bove nor below
so that growth grows
cancerously internal
ah my dead republic!

Oh city galvanic!
foundations sunk
in crab ooze in bog
its fibrous limits
filigree the green
roads shining scars
skirt sleeperless tumuli
the city lifts!
as steel tendrils tauten
we enter breathless air
two hundred thousand souls
rise from their birth beds.

Breeze over the grey Lee
history its shadow
time was streets recalled
Blarney's wry flaneur
traffic ate the time
the groves of sleep are felled.

Engineless mills
where priestwool was wound
a harvest of hands
broke rosary and rota
the hour comes with no bell
we turn on ourselves.

Cork's Lough

The kind of motion and place of the body
are determined according to the nature
of the body.
(Heidegger on Aristotle's *De caelo*)

Tangentially
the sustained crash
of metal passage
traffic
of encased bodies
liberating thissamebody
from anywhere into anywhere
a line covers nothing
this line's not-ends extend
not-yet-forever
science too slow we must learn from the artists
and accelerate

that is exchange
anything this strip of violence
but entropy but inertia but if
you can spare a time
here it curves away
into closure
(as when a line returns to itself,
that is, a body) –
here is a reserve.

Salutary round,
on the water's green girdle
easy concourse
of geese and pedestrian,
freewheeling cyclist,
recyclist, epicyclist,
past meditative anglers,
eyeing the other
element's
occluding body,
a turn of bodies
reveal at their own pace
the around-each-curve,
as the breeze enters
with hermetic birds
and the leaves utter
that once
in holiday weather
Pearse rising Corkonian Corkery:
'you'd think they'd drain it.'

Overlooking,
the 1950s

windows
are blinded,
but only kind sunshine enters
this unused hollow
to light the swans' self-ceremonies,
the parabolising tennis ball
lifted from a hurley,
metabolism
of shouts across distance
of brightness off water
of green lounging
of the birds' ascents
and descents
of the hidden source
of the island's dark thicket
setting
freedom;
so tell the roamers
that they are welcome
but there is one law:
that every carp or rudd
they pierce
and lift towards
a gasping death
must be returned to life.

Night's return
starts the mirrored illuminations
and beams lance
on the reconstituted waters,
seize momentarily
the duck's form,
the near trunk,

something on the water
in one sweep.
But the floating
swan remains
a pale cypher
and the dark island
recedes, gathers
in upon itself
a hunched obscurity.
Only stewards cross
to the moist entangled
nesting ground,
treading soft-footed around
the eggs' mottled
microcosms.
In the dead season
they place at its edge
the image of a child
in view of the city's
transposition
exposed,
open-armed
in the cold
to the firmament's
slow silent
revolution.

Angler

The rod
is my antenna,
from its tip
the long line extends
taut
to the water's surface,
descends
sensitive
into the unseen.

I wait and feel.

It comes, essentially,
to this:
attendance –
keeping light tension
between
supporting shore
and the water's possibility,
suspended,
while things pass on their way –

bird-lift from reed fringe,
the sky cloud-carrying,
hills holding
the lake's moving mirror;
in time
such things may near,
perhaps, enter…

Cast again,

openness
being never absolute,
being nothing
if not in the end:
that is,
the sudden visit,
rod galvanised and,
after play's close craft,
the speckled fish,
lured from the invisible,
there,
landed.

New Media

Time merely expanding–
the roar
of air sucked-in
after lightning.

We adapt,
locals who present
small effigies
before the altars
of the conqueror.

Strange coupling–
by night
upon the nymph,
helpless in distraction,
a bloodless Zeus
huge
descending.

Runes

I.

health
a holy well
a wet hollow

many
pending
at screens

the dead knowledge
or else
a science of death

wet leaves
pressed
glenfuls

how not to be
where you are

II.

scattered
colonies
of words

this is dry work
with little camaraderie
and Rome fallen

by the rushes
we were married
with a river for priest

word may yet come
I have gambled on its being
'amor'

spring arrives
scribbling greenery

III.

Chartres –
chrysalis
glorious glassy

neutral space –
house
fit for devils

bricks plaster
industrial paint –
the will to charity

public house
scriptorium
court of black mouths

like the sun the spirit
erring through the signs

IV.

in the world
carved away
the poem

remains
of Beuys' effort
of the artist

the ceremony ended
the doors are closed
the doors are closed

sunshine
ever enough
and fleeting

I miss Meliboeus
I miss his quiet flute at evening

V.

polaroids
of a life
worse forgotten

anything –
a prison-house
turned inside-out

the headland –
how is it
still there?

once servants
you betrayed them
you serve me

Berlin
will not be filled

VI.

Sheltered
from the sea
the harbour

withdrawn
from the harbour
the land

hidden
in the land
this

sun holding hollow.

Absent
in our exposure
to the sea

absent
in our anticipation
in the harbour

absent
in our meetings
on the land

brief
in this
sun holding hollow.

VII.

black access
shafts caves tunnels
spire's descent

estate walkways
white portico
a line of faces

autumn
unseals
branching chambers

rabbinical digit
tracks
'The Origins of Management'

in front of
an electronic portal

VIII.

'even the homeless
have time'
states Debord

such time
as is stored
in Paris Ville

the countryside
being timeless
the Cité

a timebomb
an hour-on-hour press
of anticipation

so to trading
stocks and futures

IX.

black moth
white butterfly
as missives

on the horizon
spinning
the furious top

what is not
is what is
yet to be

so a child comes
a boat approaches
presently

could time be remade
by waiting?

X.

poetry
as production
line

for an age now
art
outsourced

tiny fingers
sharp reflexes
good for such work

space
grows
in the library

as if a fire burnt
as if green things

Portraits

Elizabeth Bowen

Her face a mask,
brittle enough shell
of make-up
and restraint

Japanese
in its long-boned
economy.
She sensed

that the common art
holding body
in the sensible wear
of the 1930s

might not suffice,
nor that older effort
at Ascendancy
elegance,

considering –
the face,
even the face
might betray,

topple the person's
thin supports,
unexpectedly, one
moon-stunned evening

or in the ripples
of sex,

admit
destruction.

She knew
that features
have mould
of the tongueless howl

released
through dividing arch
at Epidauros,
and so

lest they mimic
the unconfrontable,
she assumed
this different mask

dismissive
of what for so long
pressed her shoulder,
caught

the eye's corner:
glare
of buildings' black shells
still burning

with the dawn.

This century,
her line
threading
the ruins,

brittle enough,
about the everyday,
dreamily
exact.

Her face a mask.

Beckett

The world tolls.
The sun has completed
another getting nowhere,
but it is the same
three-o-clock,
when the tabernacle
gapes.

One thing has changed:
you have taken French leave,
Rat Oboe,
and your companion,
released from tutelage
in sensitivity,
gabbles mindless
of the hour,
of the world's toll.

Nietzsche

I. Epimetheus

A great pile of notes and jottings were left on his desk—remnants and the material for his Great Project of which Zarathustra *was to have been the introductory poem.*

Forehead
like a battering ram
eyes staring and
Visigoth moustache
Buff Buff
will
that only finds expression
in explosives
Buff Buff
forehead
like a bettering ram
recalibrated again
and again to aim
higher
too many notes
until its hammer
launched
at space itself
wrenched free
too many notes
left its moorings
fell
and the great
machinery
forehead

like a battering ram
unhinged
collapsed
forest of notes
impenetrable

he was struck
dumb

It is said
that once
at a dinner party
in a childlike way
to his sister's guests
he said
'I wrote a book'

II. Philosophia

Figure it, perhaps, as a cavern –
The walls are not regular, but contain
Muscles and sinews of different stones
That grow and move, by degrees,
Over lifetimes. In the walls,
Half immersed, figures,
Caryatids, slowly lift and heave
Through stone. Gradually,
Beneath the great uplifted arms,
Bowed heads, alcoves open up.
Some, among these living pillars,
Are giants, others, sheltered
From the force of raw rock,
Toil underneath, resolve

The lesser spaces. All are connected –
The movement of one reflected
In slight repositionings elsewhere –
Ceaseless labour for new relations
With the stone. But the wall
Is not absolutely malleable:
It has its laws. And here,
Fissures and cracks have formed,

Where one, insensitive, miscalculated,
Or pushed heedlessly. As centuries pass
The cavern's hollow expands.
These words echo off the walls.

Beneath the blank expanse
Of a granite face: the fragments
Of a huge form, just recognisable,
Demolished by the effort
Of lifting what may support
The whole dome. As testament
To the massiness of the wall,
A truncated arm,
Seemingly more muscular
Broken than it could be whole,
Sinewed neck, the terrible face,
Fractured, lie.

III. Prometheus

In some backwater, where the flotsam
of history might find its way –
Dunmanway, perhaps, or Poprad, somewhere
in Estonia, prey to its own tempests

but not subject to the parent hurricanoes
and quiet now, there is a room.

It is a Sunday in early summer:
afternoon sunshine,
bright in the dust-filmed window,
flows through the old lace and continues
its slow bleaching of the bare floorboards.

The room is locked, but through its single door
come smells of cooking, the sounds
of family gathering: voices,
the scrape of a chair, doors opening and closing,
a pile of plates lifted . . .

There are few objects in this dry room –
inside the surfaces of half-peeled wallpaper,
under a bulbless light-fitting –
cardboard boxes, containing books,
a plain, deal table, to support
some jam-jars, bottles, sheets of paper.

One of these scraps: a print,
faded in the sunshine –
that face again, concentrated,
uncompromising, staring.

There are on the paper
three black, circular marks –
burnt by sunlight through a magnifying glass,
perhaps,
or bullet-holes?

XI Pieces for Austria-Hungary

1. Would you abolish the robot?
Emancipate noise?

2. Springtime in the woods,
the village voices
rise like birds.

Autumn in the capital,
the maestro orchestrates
cries of blood.

3. The search-party has occupied
the mine.
There they will uncover
the secrets of cancer.

4. Baroque
exfoliations,
falling blocks.

Far away
the brown hut
in the woods.

We cannot speak:
masonry
encrusts our tongues.

Far away
the brown hut
in the woods.

This house in disorder:
fists, tongues, ink bottles,
filling the space of breath.

Far away
the brown hut
in the woods.

5. Here, at the least,
be honest,
he told us,
as engineers.

6. A devil's art
of multiplication
to set down roots
anywhere.

A wooden machine
with steel strings
the musician's mask
to pass through boundaries.

A theatre night
in peasant's language
to excite
cartographers.

A calculator
with punch-holed cards

to list the nameless
fix no-man's-land.

7. Elements of a new geometry:
round head;
square house;
fantastic shape of a large dog.

8. Erect a tower.
Where?
Not on the ground:
the land shifts
as we shift,
the land pulls apart
if we set down.
Not in the sky:
aviators puncture
the battlements of light.
Erect a tower
there–
where the ground should be.
Erect a tower in the abyss.
And call it
Civilised Behaviour.

9. My home
a horror,
staring east:
stone gorges
four hundred years.

10. Coffeed chambers,
arabesque,
crescent pastries
before the shadowed mirror,
the gleam
on dark wood,
palms,
women

turn on themselves:
Medicine, Jurisprudence,
Art.
The state is a harem,
masterless.
Pubescents drift
among islands of flesh,
undulating hair.

11. Murder is a password
to the palace of tongues.

Various (1999–2001)

Seagull

For you
to look on
the sea
is to sense
freedom;
for my part
I walk
and it comes.

Certainly,
my way is
the more pedantic:

I
envy you your
eye,
skimming
seagull-like
across the waves.

The Quarry

The quarry spreads
and we become accustomed
to a light dust film
on everything we touch.

The quarry spreads
and where the quarry isn't
is on the road to the quarry,
the road leading from.
Here we settle,
where day opens
to the rumble of trucks,
darkness plays their lights
against our walls.

The quarry spreads
and everything
is given to activity,
every face
has the look of business.
The material transported,
the horizons hum
with the sound of construction:

what palaces are these,
greater than our ideas?
What cold, high beings
come into their own?

The Flood

So here
immersed
hung
in the flood's
obscure tumult
buffeted
by the dislodged
bodies given
to the fierce onrush
to hard downtow
our apparatus
also
loosened
floating apart
so that
as hoped for
it is like

it is like those Byzantine apostles
carriers of the word
to fresh peoples
across the border-stream's
clear babble
soul-fishers
forced to sow
new alphabets

better
it is like
those followers
words
in their mouths

already changed
feeling the Greek soil
shift underfoot
hearing
in their little Sophias
the darkening river's
swelling polyphony:

'a new Rome rises
among nomads
off all the maps;
the old Rome is transformed –
the Forum
become a cow-field,
the Tiber
a torrent of lettered stones
spilling slowly
into Gothic night.'

III Further Stepping Poems

IX.

How circumstance doth bend
our light trajectories

*

the black Zambian night
on the dust-path
hot smells
animal-voiced distances
a presence passing
close invisible

*

the body has limits
they are called generation
this world is limitless
a TV fuzz
of infinite recombination
it will be spoken
by the untongued
heartless scatter
of breath
and my brain

*

agonized leaps
screams and barks
Ernst's angel of the hearth
pulverizing dust

*

the night sky
the sky at morning

*

do you hold me
as I enter the inarticulate?
the touch so light

*

memory
unnecessary pain
like quills through skin
in a narrow access
to the underground
jammed
with fellow travellers

*

so then
not inside or outside
content or non-content
have or have not
roof peeled from a bus
rain falling on the seats

X.

Living
with the fallout
rebuilding
provisionally
gathering
each evening to watch
the flat immortals
their gestures
of lust and violence
sensing change
in the deep tissue

*

great mothercity
I am distracted
I nurture every child that comes
as if it were my child
distractedly

*

not overripe
my dear one
just florid
it is spring after all
or was

*

an anteroom
portraits
in the Goethehaus
young friends
a basket of apples
in the orchard
at dusk

*

you
you must expect
to strip
before others
you are the same
at least
we are the same
you
you are out of place
exposed

and we are smirk and muscle
excuse it!
why?
what do you hoard?

*

he made a painting of a quarry
the quarry remained
he painted the quarry
as a theatre
enduring the palm
of southern sunlight
the wall roughly stepped
with red-shafted pines
for shade
open
as if

*

grenade
pin gone
a

XI.

A quantum of unconscious
a sea of such quanta
eternal creatures in the sea
the sea in motion
intermittent making
of the same shapes
a prow above the sea
only a prow
above the sea

BANG BANG BANG
a fist on the door

*

into the clearing
where the truncated columns
resplendent
with light

*

nashhhhhhhhhunnnnahllissssssssm

*

sweet afton
and the hanging woodbine
its scent
on an evening air
breath fading
mouth of honey

*

it was in 1944 that he found a mistake in the
calculation of Pi
after place five hundred and twenty eight
it had gone awry
so he set at it
with a calculator of sorts
he recalculated
to the seven hundred and seventh place
and persisting beyond
to the eight hundred and eighth
at this point
he began to descry
a pattern
it was a unity

*

Tá brón orm, a Stiofáin,
but we're full here,
more people in the GPO
than for the last post at Christmas.
We're not doubting your spirit,
a mhic, it's just a matter of space.
Careful now
crossing the city
there'll be soldiers
and God knows what

*

what came to light
when the big house burnt?
or when that familiar stranger
one-eyed
on his pillar of establishment
came down
with a bang
what arose?
grass
muck in the yard
and where there's muck
if you're brass-necked enough
oh pass me the heuroscope
and no talk please
of cost

*

strange how buildings
might begin
as ruins
and in accelerated time

be sealed
made capsules
incapable of aging
to hold unstable
against degradation
call it luxury
that disembodied hardness
in which we age
anticipating
sudden

Various (2009 – 2010)

Ella

this
purple deity
solemn
dancing
irritated
by touch of space

daughter
apparently

or astronaut
still cordbound
to the otherworld
chancing
the outside

certainly
traveller
braver
of difficult passage
for this
manifestation
within an arm's length
not here

Idea for a New College

Green hand of spruce
in the blue air.

Cars parking,
moraine by the portico,
no branches brought
to greet the three strangers.

One brings a prism,
case for the spectrum.

Birch and spruce
10000 years,
spruce and birch
plantings,
here and there
on thin ground.

One brings a soap box
and the voice of America.

Set a fresh column
tall as a pine shaft,
new as the overalled girls,
daughters of missions.

One brings phone lines,
the news has gone out.

Beneath the bright level,
the lake is deep,
holds tools chipped from stone,
takes many streams.

We have measured the altitude
above the bright lake,
the distance is that
of here to the moon.

After J.S. Bach's *Musical Offering*

1. Canon a 2

In der Kammer in Potsdam

behind the clear
                    clock
                          face
that measures directs
courtier positions
and the State
the universe works

HERR

Rex Princeps Supremus
Majesté
Allergnädigster König

here is a problem

the fall
        through
                    coloured tones
resisting solution
halt to the old art
of canon
scandal
among the orders

herr
67 jahre
ein mann
traveller alone
in Thuringian woods

still dark enough to hold
a woodcut devil
or worse

the voice of God
from the organ-loft
bustle
      and dissonance
dutiful overlay
of unpleasing codes
compendious

thoroughgoing business
of brown things
tables, masts, beer, pens,
churches, ropes, dark bread,
chartered water

productive of girth
bürgerlich
hunched in prayer
frowns
for the grace of his children
there are ten laws
what comes not by industry
is insubstantial
its light
though the light of liberty
the light of fools

king sun

the jointed vault
may be fallen into

divine reason
lost among the stars
their singing
without cadence

I have raided the cupboard
I have gained knowledge of these things
Reinken Kepler Paracelsus

The King Laughs

and there are straight streets
wheat in the barns
unforced harmony
from Netherland to steppe
a plane stamped
by wheeling geometries
army after army

he must insist
upon his estate
a frame
thrown on grass
star-shaped
make it strong
and inside
enclearment
the obscure thicket
felled
while the law
                    leafs
                        proliferous

HERR

I have augmented
this problem
not just as notes are lengthened
(here is a multiplication of notes)
but as a king may
augment his Realme
in Rycesse, Welth, and Prosperyte
here is a wealth of difficulty

familial puzzles
the canonical ten
a fête galante
at time of departure
the old volutions
mirrors and number
returns
of Rome's failure

so the sun descends
being on a wheel
and in winter-light
fortune is tarnished
the instruments
laid out
subject of the king
become a plea

Eli Eli
canon perpetuus
ich kann nicht anders
as an offering made

2. Trio Sonata

Prussian history
not yet
absolute
there is space in the bureau
for a fluteful of breath
and its spilling over.

The doors are closed
to day's business
French windows
open
to the breeze
and to gardens
holding light
after the sun's going
from the heavens.

Now
for the light of candles
courteous
kind to artifice
so that on painted blue
the sprays of leaves
and lucent shadows
may move
in the tonic stream
unfolding and withheld
resonant in memory
in the not-yet
remembered.

It is by grace
and must be welcomed
as is natural
and a law.

Tokaji is poured
in Brandenburg crystal
with genteel words
sweet things for the ear
and before the candle ends
the clock gives measure
time like a heartbeat
and near the windows
a leaf-crowned youth
soft lustrous
on a spindle-legged chair
the sun is sitting.

From Lower Realms

A

H H

I I I

Y Y Y Y Y

Ω Ω Ω Ω Ω Ω

"... the plausible system of the heretics, which I will now describe." Irenaeus of Lyons, *Adversus Haereses.*

There are cars.
There are codes and terminals.
There is a sea that howls.
There are stars,
material fires
describing letters
at the eyes' limit.
There are three classes of men:
of clay, of flesh, and divine.
There are houses,
isolated and clustered,
in each shell
individual lives.
There are signs.
There are no rivers.
There are bushes
from other continents
planted by hotels.
There are wet periods.
There are dry periods.
There is up, down,
to the left,
to the right,
before
and behind.
There are cities
that spread like organisms.
There are organisms
that are nothing like cities.
There are churches,
mosques and meeting halls,
as many as there are prophets.

There are armies
manoeuvring by day
manoeuvring by night.
There are toothbrushes and showerheads.
There are serpents.
There is prosperity
flowing from prosperity.
There is loss.

1.

Drunkenness is dark,
complement to the fluorescent rod.

2.

"If the demiurge did not exist
he would have to be invented",
thus bringing about
a third order of creation,
the lowest
and most ungodly.

3.

By countless conduits
all corners of existence
are connected:
tunnels, vents,
drains, ducts, motorways,
tubes, corridors,
shafts, underpasses,

sewers, escalators, pipes.
Lateral angels
they minister between.
Some are lit,
and bigger than palaces,
some roar like lions
shaken by the velocity of their contents.

4.

Periodically,
though its appearance in the world
erases islands
flattens mountains
ends tribes of men,
they summon
the Tree of Knowledge.

There are cars.
There are codes and terminals.
There is a sea that howls.
There are lights
in the sky,
some move.
There are three classes of men:
of clay, of flesh, and divine.

5.

"That thought you offer
in ten centuries will reappear
grow and blossom,
to be planted

in the courtyard of the Church,
where each year
it will bear fruit;
but as it sprouts now
it is arch-heresy
a weed poisonous to stock
to be sought out
rooted up
and thrown on the fire."

6.

Los Angeles, Berlin, Lagos,
Seoul, Rome,
Sao Paulo, Jerusalem,
seven empty thrones,
from them power and condemnation,
though no man judges.

7.

Winter again,
the sun entombed,
we move to God's north.

8.

There is an ocean
not wholly contained,
where the letters lack
a fissure
scores the bed.

It is divided into zones
marked by the lines of cables
measured between the wrecks.
Some are dead,
the light fading
in green depths.
In others
a monster patrols,
gun-grey
scanning the limits.
In some
the shoals and solitaries
press all together–
the waters
like oil shifting.

9.

"But what
on the other side of death?
Why only silence
for consolation?
What valve
between?"

10.

Air
rushes into a wound
wind
blowing sparks
into outer darkness.

There are houses,
isolated and clustered,
in each shell
individual lives.
There are signs.
There are no rivers.
There is plant
and earth.
There are wet periods.
There are dry periods.
There is up, down,
to the left,
to the right,
before
and behind.

11.

Those in the know
are transported
from one heaven
to another
that is much the same.
The blind
though in motion
remain,
are nowhere.

12.

Chainsaws whining
in the beginning
violence

the Lord clearing
the fourfold woods
for the material
for the idea
for the making.

13.

"I could represent it
by tracing in the dust
that union of letters
that is emptiest
then cross it out–
that too
inadequate."

14.

This yeasty world
nearing completion
buds–
appears among the data sheets
a cosmogony.

15.

Stone
flows
slowly
like a stairs
at the base of which
a suppliant
waits

indefinitely –
about him flit
the licensed
ascending
descending.

There are cities
that spread like organisms.
There are organisms
that are nothing like cities.
There are churches,
mosques and meeting halls,
as many as there are prophets.
There are armies.

16.

"Superman, priest, genius,
all behind us,
knowledge must descend –
from general ignorance
be formed
the living Adam."

17.

The mind shuts
like a trap
God proliferates
first two
then seven
then forty-nine
then as many

as the lettered numbers
little levers
working the world of things.

18.

"Better the saved
if they must live in this world
should do so among
the contentious,
the animal-souled
subjugators of men,
than that an exalted one
in the narrow space
between serried matter
and the toss of will
should have to serve,
with a formula
beneath the tongue."

19.

Only in storms
the Beyond,
but the weather is disturbed,
the wind voices
a confusion of tongues.

20.

"We are
anticipations."

There are toothbrushes and showerheads.
There are serpents.
There is accumulation,
that repeats
and stops.

Vowels

A: Power
E: Breath
I: Extension
U: the Hook
O: Sight

A
bulldozer
incision
in a green body
lift of waters
over certainty
hammer-fall
of change

E
sustenance
of emission & exhaust
procreation's
panting mimicry
last seal
intact

O
litter
of instrument
and symbol
celestial union
of map and land
bright
font of ignorance
O horizon
fence of the squinting divine

I
reach and grasp
of simian hand
multitude of states
empire underwater
the world
again
ending

U
the hook
that replaces the robe
splice
of unmatched
struts and pipes
star-nails
of the constellations

Fergal Gaynor was born in Cork City (Ireland) in 1969, of Tipperary parents (a lecturer in Ancient Classics and a National School teacher). Educated in Cork, Sheffield, and Swansea, he was awarded a doctorate in 2002 for a thesis on D.H. Lawrence, Cézanne and modernism. Since 2000, when he co-founded the art interventionist group Art / not art, he has been continually involved in the arts, especially in his native city: performing and collaborating regularly, curating (e.g. the Cork Caucus in 2005), assisting with the SoundEye Festival, devising (e.g. The Avant: Ten Days of the Progressive Arts), editing (*ER : Enclave Review*) and writing criticism (chiefly for *Circa Contemporary Art Magazine*). He is married to the baroque violinist Marja Gaynor (née Tuhkanen) with whom he has a daughter, Eleanor.

Other titles from the Miami University Press Poetry Series

Neither World | Ralph Angel

Now | Judith Baumel

Dark Summer | Molly Bendall

Ariadne's Island | Molly Bendall

What Wind Will Do | Debra Bruce

Talk Poetry | Mairéad Byrne

Burning the Aspern Papers | John Drury

The Disappearing Town | John Drury

The Printer's Error | Aaron Fogel

Virgil's Cow | Frederick Goodwin

This Perfect Life | Kate Knapp Johnson

Wind Somewhere, and Shade | Kate Knapp Johnson

Brilliant Windows, Larry Kramer

Between Cup and Lip | Peter Manson

The Bridge of Sighs | Steve Orlen

Kisses | Steve Orlen

People Live, They Have Lives | Hugh Seidman

Selected Poems: 1965–1995 | Hugh Seidman

Long Distance | Aleda Shirley

Kingdom Come | Jim Simmerman

Moon Go Away, I Don't Love You No More | Jim Simmerman

Gender Studies | Jeffrey Skinner

Rainbow Darkness: an anthology of African American poetry | Keith Tuma, Ed.

After A Spell | Nance Van Winckel

Beside Ourselves | Nance Van Winckel

The Dirt | Nance Van Winckel